Taharah and Salah

الطهارة والصلاة – اللغة الانجليزية

Prepared by
Department of Foreigners' Awareness at Az-Zulfy

إعداد
جمعية الدعوة والإرشاد وتوعية الجاليات بالزلفي

ترجمة

Legal Rulings on Purification

Purity and Impurity

Physical Impurities: They are those that a Muslim must avoid and get rid of by washing whatever of it is on him. He must wash his clothes and body if contaminated by impurity until it is gotten rid of (until color, taste and smell of impurity are removed), if it is visible like menstrual blood for instance. However, if after the washing, some traces remain and it is difficult to get rid of it then this pardoned. On the other hand, if the impurity is invisible, it is enough to wash it even once just to get rid of it.

As for ground that has been contaminated by some impurity, it can be purified by pouring water on it. It may also be purified by drying up the impurity if it is in the form of liquid (followed by a wash). However, if it is in a solidified form, it cannot be purified except by getting rid of the impurity.

Water is used for purification and removal of impurity. This includes rainwater, seawater and other types. It is also allowed to use water that has already been used as long as it did not change its properties (color, taste, and smell). The same ruling applies to water that encountered some pure substance but remained in its original condition without changing its name from water to something else. However, it may not be used for purification if it is exposed to an impure substance that turns it into something other than water. It may not be used if contaminated with impure substances when such a substance alters its taste, smell, or color. However, if no change occurs to it after it is contaminated with impurity, the water can be used for purification according to the soundest opinion of the scholars.

The residue of water after drinking from a vessel may also be used for purification unless a dog or pig has drunk from it.

Types of Impurity

Impurities emerging from the two human bodily traces (urinary and fecal traces) are of many kinds, including:

a) Urine and feces.
b) *Al-wady*, which is the white dense fluid that is discharged after urination.
c) *Al-madhy*, which is the white sticky pre-seminal fluid discharged before the ejaculation of semen.
d) Semen, which is pure, but it is desirable to wash it off if it is moist and to scrub it off if it is dry.
e) Urine and feces of inedible animals. Urine and feces of edible animals are pure. The impurities stated

above must be washed and removed from the body and clothes affected by them except semen.
f)   Menstrual blood and postpartum bleeding.

Some Rulings Regarding Impurity:

1)   If one is affected by something, and if he is unsure whether it is impure or not, he should not enquire about it, nor must wash it, because the principle default is that all objects are pure, unless proven otherwise.

2)   When one has prayed but then notices some impurity on his body or clothes and was not aware of it before the prayer or was aware of it but forgot, his prayer is valid according to the soundest opinion of learned scholars.

3)   Anyone who cannot locate the spot of impurity on his clothes or the like should investigate and wash the part he thinks most likely to be the spot of impurity, because impurity is a tangible substance that has color, odor or taste. However, if he is unable to detect the area, which is most likely to be the spot of impurity, he should wash the whole garment.

Answering the Call of Nature:

Some etiquettes of answering the call of nature include the following:

1)   He puts forth his left foot and says the invocation before entering the toilet:

(بِسْمِ الله اللَّهُمَّ إِنِّي أَعُوذُ بِكَ مِنَ الْخُبْثِ وَالْخَبَائِثِ)

Bismil-laah allahumma innee a'oothu bika minal-khubthi wal-khaba-ith

"In the name of Allah. O Allah, I seek refuge in you from all evil and evildoers."

Upon leaving the toilet, he should say while placing forth his right foot:

(غُفْرَانَكَ) *Ghufranaka*

Meaning, "O Allah! Grant me Your forgiveness".

2) He should not have with him anything that involves the remembrance of Allah, except if he fears that it would get lost.

3) He should not face or turn his back to the direction of the *qiblah* (the Ka'bah) while urinating or defecating outdoors. As for inside buildings, he should avoid facing the *qiblah*, if possible.

4) He should be keen to cover himself and avoid allowing people to see his *'awrah*. The *'awrah* of a man is between the navel and the knee. The *'awrah* of a woman is the whole body.

5) He should avoid allowing his body or clothes to be soiled by urine or feces.

6) He should purify himself with water after answering the call of nature. He may also use tissue paper or stones and the like to get rid of the impurity, and he should use the left hand while cleansing himself.

Ablution (*Wudu'*)

Prayer is not accepted without purification. On the authority of Abu Hurairah (may Allah be pleased with him), the Messenger of Allah (May the blessings and peace of Allah be upon him) said, *"Indeed, Allah does not accept the prayer (Salaah) of any of you when he violates the ablution unless he has performed ablution"*. [Agreed upon: 6954, 225]

Moreover, maintaining order and continuity (*At-Tarteeb* and *Al-Muwaalaat*) [1] of wudu' must be taken into account while making it.

There are many great virtues associated with ablution, which we should be aware of. They include the following:

Uthman bin 'Affan reported that the Messenger of Allah (May the blessings and peace of Allah be upon him) said, **"Whoever performs ablution in the right**

---

(1) *At-Tarteeb* is for one to arrange the washing of the bodily organs sequentially This is achieved by washing the face, then the two hands; then he wipes over the head and both ears and then washes the feet.

Al-Muwaalaat is for one not to leave a long time gap between the washing of an organ and the other by allowing one organ to get dry before commencing the washing of the next organ.

manner will have his sins leave his body until they come out from under his nails."

He also narrated that the Messenger of Allah (May the blessings and peace of Allah be upon him) said, *"Whoever performs ablution perfectly as Allah has ordained, the obligatory prayers he observes after that would be an expiation of the sins he committed between these prayers."* [Transmitted by Muslim: 231].

How to Perform Ablution

1. He makes intention in his mind without saying it loud with his tongue. Intention means the resolution of the heart to do anything. Then he should say, (بسم الله)

Bismillaah, which means: (In the Name of Allah)
2. Then he washes his hands thrice.
3. Then he rinses his mouth, inhales water into his nostrils, and blows it out three times.
4. Then he washes his face three times starting from one ear to the other widthwise and from the forehead down to below the chin lengthwise.
5. Then he washes his arm thrice starting from the finger edges and including the elbow. He begins with the right hand and then the left.
6. Then he wipes his head once by wetting his palms with water and then runs them over his head starting

from the forehead to the rear end of the head and then returns with them to the forehead again.

7. Then he wipes his ears once by putting his index fingers into the meatus of the ears and wiping the outer parts of his ears with the thumbs.

8. Then he washes his legs thrice starting from the toe edges including the two ankles. He begins by the right leg before the left one.

9. It is desirable to say the following invocation that was recorded from the Prophet (May the blessings and peace of Allah be upon him): "*Ash-Hadu al-Laa Ilaaha Illallaah Wa Ash-Hdu Anna Muhammadan Abduhu wa Rasuluh*", which means: I testify that there is no deity worthy of worship except Allah and I testify that Muhammad is His slave and Messenger.

On the authority of Umar bin Al-Khattab (May Allah be pleased with him), the Messenger of Allah (May the blessings and peace of Allah be upon him) said,

No one would perform ablution perfectly and then says, I testify that there is no deity worthy of worship except Allah and I testify that Muhammad is His slave and Messenger, but would have the eight gates of the Paradise opened for him and he may enter by whichever of them he wishes. [Transmitted by Muslim: 234].

How to Perform Wudu

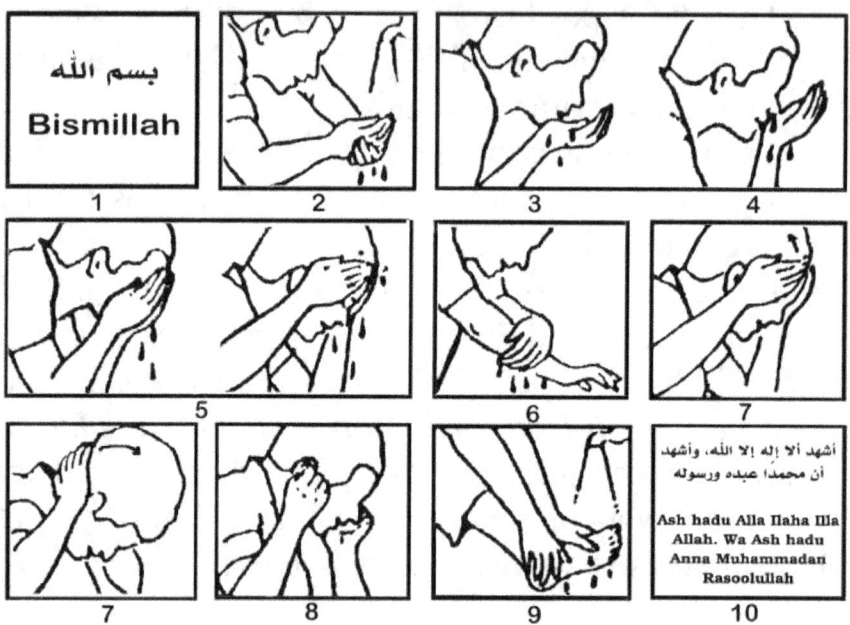

Wiping over the socks

It is part of the magnanimity and simplicity of Islam that it permits for one to wipe over the socks. This is what has been confirmed from the Prophet (May the blessings and peace of Allah be upon him) on the authority of 'Amr bin Umayyah (May Allah be pleased with him) who said, *"I saw the Prophet (May the blessings and peace of Allah be upon him) wiping over his turban and Khuff (socks)."* [Transmitted by Al-Bukhari: 205].

Al-Mughirah bin Shu'bah (May Allah be pleased with him) reported saying, "Once upon a night, I was with the Messenger of Allah (May the blessings and peace of Allah be upon him), he descended and relieved himself. Then he returned and I poured water for him from a kettle that was with me. So he performed ablution and wiped over his *khuff* (leather socks)." [Agreed upon: 203, 274]

However, it is required for one to put on the *khuff* (leather socks) in a state of purity before wiping over them.
- In other words, he should perform ablution before wearing them.
- He wipes over them by running his wet hand over them from above. He should not wipe underneath them.
- One day and one night (24 hours) have been specified for someone who is a resident, while three days and nights (72 hours) have been stipulated for the traveler who is on a lawful journey that allows him to shorten his prayers.
- Wiping becomes invalid as soon as the fixed period of wiping expires or when he removes them after having wiped over them, or when he is in the state of major impurity (*janabah*), whereby it becomes mandatory for him to pull them off so that he may take a ritual bath (*ghusl*).

Invalidators of Ablution

1. Discharge from the two human urinary and fecal traces including urine, stool, wind, semen, pre-seminal fluid, al-wadi, which is the white dense fluid that is discharged after urination, and blood.
2. Sleep.
3. Consuming camel meat.
4. Falling unconscious or when one loses his senses.

The Ritual Bath (*Al-Ghusl*)

Al-Ghusl is the act of pouring water all over the body with the intention of purification. It cannot be sound without washing the whole body, including rinsing the mouth and inhaling and exhaling water in and out the nostrils. A ritual bath (*ghusl*) becomes obligatory for five reasons, and they are as follows:

Firstly: The discharge of semen with sexual desire from a male or the discharge of sexual fluid (expelled during orgasm) for a female while awake or asleep. If the semen is discharged without sexual desire, such as when it is discharged because of a sickness or intensive cold, a ritual bath would not be compulsory. Similarly, if one dreams but he does not find any traces of semen, a ritual bath is not obligatory. However, if he finds any traces of semen, he must take a ritual bath even though he cannot recollect any dreams.

Secondly: Physical contact between the male and female sexual organs as long as penetration occurs and even if no semen is discharged.

Thirdly: Termination of menstrual or postpartum bleeding.

Fourthly: Death, whereby it becomes obligatory to wash the corpse.

Fifthly: Upon the reversion of an unbeliever to Islam, he must take a ritual bath.

Things prohibited for one in a state of major impurity

Major impurity is a state that occurs to a man or woman when copulation occurs or when the semen or female sexual fluid (expelled at orgasm) is discharged accompanied by sexual desire even if no copulation has occurred or when the semen or female sexual fluid is discharged during a wet dream. There are certain activities prohibited upon someone who is in a state of major impurity (*janabah*) including:

1- Prayer (*Salaah*).
2- Circumambulation of the Ka'bah (*Tawaf*).
3- Direct contact of the body with a copy of the holy Qur'an (*Al-Mushaf*) without any barrier. It is also prohibited to recite the Glory Qur'an in an audible or

inaudible voice, whether from memory or from a copy of the Qur'an and the like.

4- Staying in the mosque. There are no qualms in passing through it, and a person may stay in the mosque if there is a need for that, but he must erase the state of his impurity by performing ablution.

The Alternative of Ablution or Ritual Bath (*At-Tayammum*)

Tayammum is permissible while one is a resident or on a journey. It is the alternative to both ablution and the ritual bath when any of the following reasons is found:

1- In the absence of water or when there is water but it is not adequate for purification. Although, this should not be resorted to except after seeking and making a serious quest for water first. He can then perform *tayammum* if he does not find water or even if there is water close to him but he fears for his life or some harm occurring to him if he goes to fetch it.

2- If some body part of ablution is injured and will be harmed by washing it, he should wipe over it by wetting his hand with water and running it over the injured body part. However, if wiping is also harmful to him, he should wash the other parts normally and perform *tayammum* for the injured part.

3- When the water or weather is intensively cold and he fears incurring some harm when he uses the water (and he cannot heat it) he can perform *tayammum*.

4- When he has a little bit of water but he requires it for drinking or cooking, he can perform *tayammum*.

How to Perform *Tayammum*

He should make intention in his mind and strike his palms on the earth once. Then he wipes his face, then wipes the exterior part of his right hand with the palm of the left hand, and then wipes the exterior part of his left hand with the palm of the right hand.

Tayammum becomes invalid through the same things that make ablution invalid. It also becomes invalid upon the availability of water for one who could not find it before or during the Prayer (*Salaah*). However, his prayer remains valid and he does not have to repeat it if he finds water after he has already prayed.

Menstruation and Postpartum Bleeding

Menstruation (*Al-Haidw*) is the blood that is discharged at a state of sound health from the innermost part of a woman's uterus for a specific period and it is not due to childbirth or sickness. It is usually dark in color and has an odor.

Post-Partum Bleeding (*An-Nifas*) is the blood that is discharged from a woman's uterus because of childbirth.

A woman in a state of menstruation or postpartum bleeding is prohibited from praying or fasting while in that state, as mentioned in the hadith of Aishah (may Allah be pleased with her). The Messenger of Allah (May the blessings and peace of Allah be upon him) said, "When the menstrual blood begins, leave the Prayer – *Salaah*, and **when it stops, wash off the blood from you and pray.**" [Agreed upon 331, 333].

A menstruating woman is not obliged to make up the missed prayers. However, she is obliged to make up the days she missed fasting during Ramadan. Moreover, it is not permissible for her to circumambulate the Ka'bah. Sexual intercourse is not allowed during her period, though other acts of intimacy besides sexual intercourse are allowed. It is

Taharah and Salah

also not permissible for the menstruating woman to touch a copy of the Glorious Qur'an.

A woman in menses becomes pure when the bleeding stops, and she must take a ritual bath before all the activities that were forbidden to her become lawful.

When a woman experiences menses or post-partum bleeding after the setting in of the time of prayer and but she did not observe that prayer, the correct opinion is that she has to make up for that prayer once she is pure. When a woman is purified before the expiration of the prayer time by the period of one rak'ah (one unit of prayer), it is obligatory on her to observe that prayer. However, it is desirable for her to make up for the prayer that is usually combined with that prayer. For instance, if she gets pure before sunset, it is obligatory for her to pray 'Asr and desirable for her to pray Dhuhr also. Moreover, if she becomes clean before midnight, she should pray 'Isha and it is desirable for her to make up Maghrib prayer as well.

Legal Rulings on Prayer (Salaah)

Prayer (*Salaah*) is the second pillar of Islam. It is obligatory on every sane and mature Muslim.

Maturity occurs by the attainment of the age of fifteen, or the growth of the pubic hair, or discharge of the semen through a wet dream or other means. Females have an additional sign of maturity, which is menstrual bleeding. Hence, whenever a person experiences any of these signs, he has attained adulthood and the age of maturity.

Any one who denies the obligation of Prayer (*Salaah*) has rejected Islam according to the consensus of the scholars. As regards to the one who abandons the prayer out of remissness or laziness, the Companions of the Prophet (May the blessings and peace of Allah be upon him) are of consensus that he has disbelieved.

Prayer is the first act for which the slave of Allah will be held accountable on the Day of Judgment. Allah the Most High said,

﴿ إِنَّ الصَّلاةَ كَانَتْ عَلَى الْمُؤْمِنِينَ كِتَاباً مَوْقُوتاً ﴾ [النساء: ١٠٣]

"Prayer (*Salaah*) has been enjoined on the believers at fixed hours." [An-Nisa: 103]

On the authority of Ibn Umar (May Allah be pleased with him), the Prophet (May the blessings and peace of Allah be upon him) said, *"Islam is based on five (principles): to testify that none has the right to be worshipped but Allah and Muhammad is Allah's Messenger, to offer the (compulsory congregational) prayers dutifully and perfectly, to pay Zakaah (i.e. obligatory charity), to perform Hajj. (i.e. Pilgrimage to Makkah), to observe fast during the month of Ramadan."* [Agreed upon: 6, 18].

Jabir bin Abdullah, (May Allah be pleased with him), narrated, "I heard the Messenger (May the blessings and peace of Allah be upon him) say, *'Between man, polytheism, and disbelief is the abandonment of prayer.'*" [Transmitted by Muslim: 82]
Moreover, there are many great virtues associated with the observance of prayer. These include what Abu Hurairah (May Allah be pleased with him) narrated that the Messenger of Allah (May the blessings and peace of Allah be upon him) said, "He that purifies himself at home and then walks to any house – mosque, of the houses of Allah –, in order to perform some obligation of the obligations of Allah, will have one of his footsteps wipe of sin and the other elevate him a grade above" [Transmitted by Muslim: 666].

He also reported that the Messenger of Allah (May the blessings and peace of Allah be upon him) said, *"Should I guide you to that by which Allah wipes sins and elevates in status?"* They replied, *'Of course O Messenger of Allah.'* He said, *"Performing ablution properly at times when it is difficult to do so, taking many steps to the masjid, and waiting for a prayer after a prayer. That is your ribaat – (i.e. guarding the frontier)."*

He further narrated from the Prophet (May the blessings and peace of Allah be upon him) that he said, *"He who goes to the masjid at dawn or dusk (for prayer), Allah prepares a hospitable abode for him in Jannah; every time when he walks to it or comes back from it".* [Agreed upon: 662, 669]

Some Important Issues Related to Prayer:
1. Congregational prayer is obligatory for men in the mosque according to the Hadith, **"I sometimes thought of giving orders for proclaiming the *Adhan* for *Salaah*. Then I would go to the houses of those who do not come to perform *Salaah* in congregation, and set their houses ablaze on them."**
2. It is required of a Muslim to come to the mosque early with tranquility and calmness.
3. It is a desirable act of Sunna*h* for anyone entering the mosque to enter with his right foot, saying the

reported invocation: (اللّٰهُمَّ افْتَحْ لِي أَبْوابَ رَحْمَتِك), *"Allahumma iftah lee abwaba rahmatik"*, meaning "O Allah, open the gates of Your mercy for me." [Transmitted by Muslim: 1652]

4. It is also an act of Sunnah for him to observe two *rak'ahs* (units of prayer) before sitting in the masjid, as mentioned in the *hadith* of Abu Qatadah (May Allah be pleased with him) that the Messenger of Allah (may the blessings and peace of Allah be upon him) said, ***"If any of you enters a mosque, he should pray two rak'ahs before sitting."*** [Agreed upon: 444, 714]

5. He must cover his *'awrah* (nudity) before prayer. The *'awrah* of a man is between the navel and the knee and that of a woman is all her body except the face.

6. It is obligatory to face the direction of the *Qiblah* (Ka'bah in Makkah) and it is a basic requirement for the acceptance of prayer except in two situations: existence of some impediment such as sickness and the like, and while traveling (such as in the car or airplane or on a riding animal). However, this circumstance is restricted to the supererogatory prayers only.

7. It is mandatory to observe the prayers on time, because prayer is not valid before its specific timing and it is prohibited to delay it after its appointed time.

8. It is from the Prophet's *Sunnah* to go early for prayer, to be keen on praying in the first row, and to wait for the prayer before it is performed. On the

authority of Abu Hurairah, (May Allah be pleased with him), the Messenger of Allah (May the blessings and peace of Allah be upon him) said: **"*Were people to know the blessing of making the a*dhan and the standing in the first row, they would even draw lots to secure these privileges. And were they to realize the reward of performing *Salaah* early, they would race for it; ..."** [Agreed upon: 615, 437].

Abu Hurairah also reported that the Messenger of Allah (May the blessings and peace of Allah be upon him) said, **"Everyone among you will be deemed to be busy with *Salaah* (prayer) constantly so long as *Salaah* (the prayer) detains him (from worldly concerns)..."** [Transmitted by Al-Bukhari and Muslim: 659, 649]

Prayer Times

- The time for *Dhuhr* starts from when the sun passes the meridian (declines) until when everything becomes equal (to the length of) its shadow (excluding the shadwow present at zenith).
- The time for *Asr* starts from when everything becomes similar (to the length of) its shadow (excluding the shadow at zenith) until the sun sets.
- The time for *Maghrib* starts from when the sun has set until when the red twilight has vanished, which is the reddish glow that succeeds the sunset.

- The time for *Isha* starts from when the red twilight has vanished until midnight.
- The time for *Fajr* starts from when *Fajr* (dawn) begins until sunrise.

Places where prayer (*Salaah*) is not valid

1. Graveyards, due to the saying of Prophet Muhammad (May the blessings and peace of Allah be upon him), **"The whole earth is a place of prayer except public baths and graveyards."** [Sound tradition, transmitted by the five transmitters of Hadith viz: Al-Bukhari, Muslim, Abu Dawud, At-Tirmidhi and An-Nasa'ee]
2. Observing prayer (*Salaah*) facing a grave. Abu Marthad Al-Ghanawy (May Allah be pleased with him) said, "I heard the Messenger of Allah (May the blessings and peace of Allah be upon him) saying: **'Do not offer *Salaah* (prayer) facing the graves and do not sit on them.'"** [Transmitted by Muslim: 973].
3. Camel barns or other dwellings and shelters for camels.
4. It is also not allowed to perform prayer in impure places.

How the Prayer is Observed

Intention must be called to mind during prayer and before all acts of worship. The intention is made in the mind and must not be proclaimed by the tongue. Prayer is performed as follows:

1. The person observing prayer faces the Qiblah direction with all his body and without any deviation or turning around here and there.

2. Then he makes the *Takbeeratul-Ihraam* (opening *Takbeer*) saying: (الله أكبر) - *Allahu akbar*, meaning: Allah is the Greatest. He raises his hands to the level of his shoulders or ears while saying the *Takbeer*.

3. Then he places his right palm on the outer part of his left palm and puts then on his chest.

4. Then he says the opening invocation (*Du'a Al-Istiftaah*) – (الحمد لله حمداً كثيراً طيباً مباركاً فيه) - *Alhamdu lillahi hamdan katheeran tayyiban mubarakan feeh*, meaning: *"Allah be praised with an abundant beautiful blessed praise."* [Transmitted by Muslim: 600].

Alternatively, he may say,

(سبحانك اللّهمّ وبحمدِك وتبارك اسمُك وتعالى جدُّك ولا إلهَ غيرُك)

Subhanakal-lahumma wabihamdika watabarakas-muka wata'Aala jadduka wala ilaha ghayruk,

Taharah and Salah

Meaning: How perfect You are O Allah, and I praise You. Blessed be Your Name, and lofty is Your position and none has the right to be worshipped except You.' [Transmitted by Abu Dawud and At-Tirmidhi: 775, 242 and graded Sahih by Al-Albani]. He may say any other invocation of opening. However, it is preferred for him to diversify and not perpetuate on one invocation as that is more likely to cause him humility and consciousness in prayer.

5. Then he seeks refuge in Allah saying, أعوذ بالله من الشيطان الرجيم *A'udhu billahi minash-shaytanir-rajeem*,

Meaning: 'I take refuge with Allah from the accursed devil.'

6. Then he says, (بسم الله الرحمن الرحيم) – *Bismillahir-Rahmanir-Rahim*,

Meaning: In the Name of Allah, the most Gracious, the most Compassionate.

The he recites Surah Al-Fatihah:

﴿ بِسْمِ اللَّهِ الرَّحْمَنِ الرَّحِيمِ (١) الْحَمْدُ لِلَّهِ رَبِّ الْعَالَمِينَ (٢) الرَّحْمَنِ الرَّحِيمِ (٣) مَالِكِ يَوْمِ الدِّينِ (٤) إِيَّاكَ نَعْبُدُ وَإِيَّاكَ نَسْتَعِينُ (٥) اهْدِنَا الصِّرَاطَ الْمُسْتَقِيمَ (٦) صِرَاطَ الَّذِينَ أَنْعَمْتَ عَلَيْهِمْ غَيْرِ الْمَغْضُوبِ عَلَيْهِمْ وَلَا الضَّالِّينَ (٧) ﴾ آمين

(1) In the Name of Allah, the Most Gracious, the Most Merciful.(2) All Praise is due and belongs to Allah, the Cherisher and Sustainer of the worlds ؛ (3)

The Most Gracious, the Most Merciful (4) Master of the Day of Judgment.(5) It is You do we worship, and You we seekfor aid.(6) Show us the straight way‹(7) The way of those on whom You have bestowed Your Grace, not of those whose (portion) is wrath, nor those who go astray.   Ameen.

7. Then he recites whatever is possible from the Qur'an.

8. Then he bows raising his hands to the level of his shoulders saying, (اللهُ أَكْبَرَ) - *Allahu akbar*, meaning: Allah is the Greatest.

While in the *Ruku'* position, he places his palms on his knees with the fingers spread out and he says, (سُبْحانَ رَبِّيَ الْعَظيم) -*Subhana rabbiyal-'Atheem*, meaning:'How perfect my Lord is, The Supreme.'

The established practice (*Sunnah*) is to say it three times, though he may do more than that but it suffices if he says it once.

9. Then he raises his head from the bowing (*Ruku'*) position saying, (for both the Imam and the one praying alone) while he raises his hands to the level of his shoulders while rising from the bowing position,

(سَمِعَ اللهُ لِمَنْ حَمِدَه)

Sami'a Al-laahu liman hamidah –
Meaning: ' May Allah answer he who praises Him.'

Taharah and Salah 27

In lieu of (سَمِعَ اللهُ لِمَنْ حَمِدَه) both the person led and the one praying alone say the invocation (رَبَّنَا وَلَكَ الْحَمْدُ) - *Rabbana walakal-hamdu*, meaning: 'Our Lord, for You is all praise.

He places his right palm on the outer part of his left palm on his chest.

10. While standing, he says,

((اللَّهُمَّ رَبَّنَا لَكَ الْحَمْدُ ، مِلْءَ السَّمَاوَاتِ وَمِلْءَ الْأَرْضِ وَمِلْءَ مَا بَيْنَهُمَا ، وَمِلْءَ مَا شِئْتَ مِنْ شَيْءٍ بَعْدُ)) [رواه مسلم: ٧٧١]

Allahumma Rabbana lakal-hamduMil-as-samawati wamil-al-ard, wama baynahuma, wamil/a ma shi'ta min shay-in ba'du, Meaning:

'O' Allah our Lord, for You is all praise, the heavens and the Earth and all between them abound with Your praises, and all that You will abounds with Your praises. [Transmitted by Muslim: 771].

11. Then he prostrates the first prostration saying while doing it: (اللهُ أَكْبَر) - *Allahu akbar*, meaning: Allah is the Greatest.

He should prostrate on his seven organs: the forehead with the nose, the two hands, knees and edges of the feet. He should give gap between his brachia and side arms allowing the tip of his toes face the Qiblah direction. During prostration he says: (سُبْحَانَ رَبِّيَ الْأَعْلَى)

Subhana rabbiyal-A'la, meaning: 'How perfect my Lord is, The Most High.'

The established practice (*Sunnah*) of the Prophet (May the blessings and peace of Allah be upon him) is to say it three times, though he may do more than that, but saying it once suffices.

It is desirable to make frequent invocations during prostration; as it is one of the positions where prayer is likely to be answered.

12. Then he lifts his head from prostration (*Sujood*) saying: (اللهُ أَكْبَر) - *Allahu akbar*, meaning: Allah is the Greatest, and sits between the two prostrations on his left foot, keeping his right foot erect, placing his right hand on the tip of his right thigh, which is near to the Knee, and putting his left hand on the tip of his left thigh, which is near to the knee stretchinghis fingers while sitting and saying, (رَبِّ اغْفِرْ لِي ، رَبِّ اغْفِرْ لِي) *Rabbigh-fir lee, rabbigh-fir lee*, meaning: 'My Lord forgive me, My Lord forgive me.'

13. Then he prostrates for the second prostration, and does as he did in the first prostration.

14. Then he rises from the second prostration saying, (اللهُ أَكْبَر) - *Allahu Akbar*, meaning: Allah is the Greatest,and stands upright.

15. He observes the second *rak'ah* just as he did in the first regarding the actions and sayings, but he does not read the opening *du'aa* nor seeks refuge from the accursed devil. After the second prostration of the

second *rak'ah*, he sits as he had sit between the two prostrations, but will have to grip the fingers of his right hand holding the thumb with the central finger and pointing with the forefinger. He should recite the *Tashahhud* while sitting, saying,

((التَّحِيَّاتُ لله ، والصَّلَوَاتُ والطيِّبَاتُ ، السَّلاَمُ عَلَيْكَ أَيُّهَا النبيُّ وَرَحْمَةُ الله وبَرَكَاتُهُ، السَّلاَمُ عَلَيْنَا وعَلَى عِبَادِ الله الصَّالِحِينَ، أَشْهَدُ أَنْ لا إلهَ إلا الله، وأَشْهَدُ أَنَّ مُحَمَّداً عَبْدُهُ وَرَسُولُهُ)) [رواه البخاري: ٨٣١]

Attahiyyatu lillahi wassalawatu wattayyibat, assalamu 'Alayka ayyuhan-nabiyyu warahmatul-lahi wabarakatuh, assalamu 'Alayna wa'Ala ibadil-lahis-saliheen. Ash-hadu al-la ilaha illal-lah, wa-ashhadu anna Muhammadan Abduhu warasooluh,

Meaning:

At-tahiyyat[1] is for Allah. All acts of worship and good deeds are for Him. Peace, mercy and blessings of Allah be upon you O Prophet. Peace be upon us and all of Allah's righteous servants. I bear witness that none has the right to be worshipped except Allah and I bear witness that Muhammad is His slave and Messenger'. [Transmitted by Al-Bukhari: 831]. There are some other forms of Tashahhud besides this.

---

(1) At-Tahiyyat means all words which indicate the glorification of Allah, His eternal existence, His perfection and His sovereignty.

If he is offering a prayer of three *rak'ahs* such as *Maghrib* or four *rak'ahs* such as *Ad-Dhuhr* or *Al-Asr* or *Al-'Isha* prayer she rises for the third rak'ah saying, (الله أكْبَر) - *Allahu Akbar*, meaning: Allah is the Greatest. He should raise his hands to the level of his shoulders while rising. Then he completes the remaining part of his prayer in the same manner he observed the second *rak'ah* except that he would only recite Surah Al-Fatihah while standing. After the second prostration of the last *rak'ah*, he should sit and recite the *Tashahhud* and *As-Salaah Al-Ibrahimiyyah* (Abrahamic invocation):

((التَّحِيَّاتُ لله ، والصَّلَوَاتُ والطيِّبَاتُ ، السَّلاَمُ عَلَيْكَ أَيُّهَا النبيُّ وَرَحْمَةُ الله وبَرَكَاتُهُ، السَّلامُ عَلَيْنَا وعَلَى عِبَادِ الله الصَّالِحِينَ، أَشْهَدُ أَنْ لا إلَهَ إلا الله، وأَشْهَدُ أَنَّ مُحَمَّداً عَبْدُهُ ورَسُولُهُ، اللَّهُمَّ صَلِّ عَلَى مُحَمَّدٍ ، وَعَلَى آلِ مُحَمَّدٍ، كَمَا صَلَّيْتَ عَلَى إبراهيم وَعَلَى آلِ إِبْرَاهِيمَ، إنَّكَ حَمِيدٌ مَجِيدٌ ، اللهم بَارِكْ عَلَى مُحَمَّدٍ، وعَلَى آلِ مُحَمَّدٍ ، كَمَا بَارَكْتَ عَلَى إِبْرَاهِيمَ ، وَعَلَى آلِ إِبْرَاهِيمَ ، إنَّكَ حَمِيدٌ مَجِيدٌ)).

Attahiyyatu lillahi wassalawatu wattayyibat, assalamu 'alayka ayyuhan-nabiyyu warahmatul-lahi wabarakatuh, assalamu 'alayna wa 'ala 'ibadil-lahis-saliheen. Ash-hadu al-la ilaha illa Allah, wa-ashhadu anna Muhammadan 'abduhu warasooluh, All<u>a</u>humma s<u>a</u>lli 'al<u>a</u> Muh<u>a</u>mmad, wa-'al<u>a</u> <u>a</u>ali Muh<u>a</u>mmad, kam<u>a</u>sallayta 'al<u>a</u> Ibr<u>a</u>heema wa-'al<u>a</u> <u>a</u>ali Ibr<u>a</u>heem, innaka <u>H</u>ameedun Majeed, All<u>a</u>humma b<u>a</u>rik 'al<u>a</u> Muh<u>a</u>mmad, wa-'al<u>a</u> <u>a</u>ali Muh<u>a</u>mmad, kam<u>a</u> b<u>a</u>rakta *ala Ibraheema wa-'ala aali Ibraheem, innaka Hameedun Majeed.*

Meaning: *"Greetings are for Allah. All acts of worship and good deeds are for Him. Peace and the mercy and blessings of Allah be upon you O Prophet. Peace be upon us and all of Allah's righteous servants. I bear witness that none has the right to be worshipped except Allah, and I bear witness that Muhammad is His slave and Messenger. O Allah, send prayers upon Muhammad and the followers of Muhammad, just as You sent prayers upon Ibraheem and upon the followers of Ibraheem. Verily, You are full of praise and majesty. O Allah, send blessings upon Muhammad and upon the family of Muhammad, just as You sent blessings upon Ibraheem and upon the family of Ibraheem. Verily, You are full of praise and majesty."*

Following this, he makes any invocation he may wish and it is the established practice of the Prophet (May the blessings and peace of Allah be upon him) to make frequent invocations, saying the recorded invocations from the Sunnah:

((اللَّهُمَّ إِنِّي أَعُوذُ بِكَ مِنْ عَذَابِ الْقَبْرِ، وَمِنْ عَذَابِ النَّارِ، وَمِنْ فِتْنَةِ المَحْيَا وَالمَمَاتِ، وَمِنْ فِتْنَةِ المَسِيحِ الدَّجَّالِ))

Allahumma innee a'udhu bika min 'adhabil-qabr, wamin 'adhabin-naar, wamin fitnatil-mahya walmamat, wamin fitnatil-maseehid-dajjal, meaning:

"O Allah, I seek refuge in You from the punishment of the grave, from the torment of the Fire, from the trials and tribulations of life and death and from the affliction of Al-Maseeh Ad-Dajjal (the Anti-Christ)."

16. Then make *tasleem* (concluding act of the prayer) to the right saying, (السَّلامُ عَلَـيْكُمْ ورَحمة الله) - *Assalamu 'A'laykum Wa Rahmatullaah,* meaning: "Peace and mercy of Allah be upon you", and then to the left likewise.

17. During the final *tashahhud* of *Dhuhr, Asr, Maghrib,* and *'Isha* prayers, it is an established practice of the Prophet to sit in the position of *tawarruk,* which is to sit on your left leg, propping up his right foot so that the tips of his toes are on the ground, facing the Qiblah, and taking his left foot out from under his right leg, and positioning both his arms as he did during the *Tashahhud.*

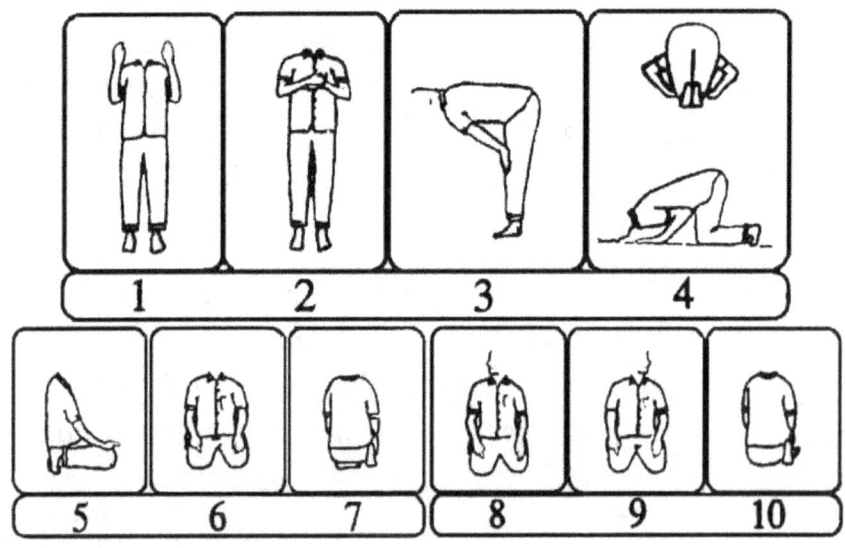

Remembrance of Allah (*Adhkaar*) to be said after the Prayer

أَسْتَغْفِرُ اللهَ ، أَسْتَغْفِرُ اللهَ ، أَسْتَغْفِرُ اللهَ ، اللَّهُمَّ أَنْتَ السَّلَامُ وَمِنْكَ السَّلَامُ ،

تَبَارَكْتَ يَا ذَا الْجَلَالِ وَالْإِكْرَامِ

Astaghfirul-lah, Astaghfirul-lah, Astaghfirul-lah, Allahumma antas-salam waminkas-salam, tabarakta ya dhal-jalali wal-ikram.

"I ask Allah for forgiveness, I ask Allah for forgiveness, I ask Allah for forgiveness. O Allah, You are As-Salam (i.e. the One Who is free from all defects and deficiencies) and from You is all peace, blessed are You, O' Possessor of majesty and honour." [Transmitted by Muslim: 591].

لَا إِلَهَ إِلَّا اللهُ وَحْدَهُ لَا شَرِيكَ لَهُ ، لَهُ الْمُلْكُ ، وَلَهُ الْحَمْدُ ، وَهُوَ عَلَى كُلِّ شَيْءٍ قَدِيرٌ ،

اللَّهُمَّ لَا مَانِعَ لِمَا أَعْطَيْتَ ، وَلَا مُعْطِيَ لِمَا مَنَعْتَ ، وَلَا يَنْفَعُ ذَا الْجَدِّ مِنْكَ الْجَدّ

La ilaha illal-lahu wahdahu la shareeka lah, lahul-mulku walahul-hamd, wahuwa 'ala kulli shayin qadeer, allahumma la mani'a lima a'atayt, wala mu'tiya lima mana't, wala yanfa'u dhal-jaddi minkal-jad.

"None has the right to be worshipped except Allah, alone, without partner, to Him belongs all sovereignty and praise and He is over all things omnipotent. O' All*a*h, none can prevent what You have willed to bestow and none can bestow what You have willed to prevent, and no wealth or majesty can benefit anyone, as from You is all wealth and majesty." [Agreed upon: 844, 593].

لاَ إلهَ إلاَّ اللهُ وَحْدَهُ لاَ شَـرِيكَ لَهُ ، لَهُ الْمُلْكُ ، وَلَهُ الْحَمْـدُ ، وَهُوَ عَلى كُلِّ شَيءٍ قَدِيرٌ، لاَ حَوْلَ وَلاَ قُوَّةَ إلاَّ بِاللهِ ، لاَ إلهَ إلاَّ اللهُ ، ولاَ نَعبُدُ إلاَّ إيَّاهُ ، لهُ النِّعمَةُ ولهُ الفَضْلُ ، ولهُ الثنَاءُ الحَسَنُ ، لاَ إلهُ إلاَّ اللهُ مُخْلِصينَ لهُ الدِّينَ ولو كَرِهَ الكَافِرونَ

La ilaha illal-lah, wahdahu la shareeka lah, lahul-mulku walahul-hamd, wahuwa 'ala kulli shayin qadeer. Lahawla wala quwwata illa billah, la ilaha illal-lah, wala na'budu illa iyyah, lahun-ni'matu walahul-fadl walahu thana-ul- hasan, la ilaha illa Allah mukhliseena lahud-deen walaw karihal-kafiroon.

"None has the right to be worshipped except All*a*h, alone, without partner, to Him belongs all sovereignty and praise, and He is over all things omnipotent. There is no might or power except with All*a*h, none has the right to be worshipped except All*a*h and we worship none except Him. For Him is all favour, grace, and glorious praise. None has the right to be worshipped except All*a*h, and we are sincere in faith and devotion to Him even if the disbelievers detest it." [Transmitted by Muslim: 594].

Taharah and Salah

Following this, he says (thirty three times each), (سُبْحانَ الله) - *Subhanal-lah*, meaning: "How perfect Allah is."

(الْحَمْدُ لله) - *Alhamdu lillah*, meaning: "All praise is due and belongs to Allah."

(اللهُ أَكْبَر) – *Allahu Akbar*, meaning: "Allah is the Greatest."

Then he completes the hundred by saying,

لاَ إِلهَ إِلاَّ اللهُ وَحْدَهُ لاَ شَرِيكَ لَهُ ، لَهُ الْمُلْكُ ، وَلَهُ الْحَمْدُ ، وَهُوَ عَلَى كُلِّ شَيْءٍ قَدِيرٌ

La ilaha illa Allah wahdahu la shareeka lah, lahul-mulku walahul-hamd, wahuwa 'ala kulli shay'in qadeer.

"None has the right to be worshipped except Allah, alone, without a partner, to Him belongs all sovereignty and praise and He is over all things omnipotent." [Transmitted by Muslim: 597].

He should also recite *Aayatul-Kursiyy* (verse 255 of the Glorious Qur'an) and the following chapters after every prayer. However, it is desirable to repeat the three chapters thrice after *Fajr* and *Maghrib* prayers:

﴿ قُلْ هُوَ اللهُ أَحَدٌ ..... ﴾

{*Qul huwa Allahu ahad...*}   [Surah Al-Ikhlas]

﴿قُلْ أَعُوذُ بِرَبِّ الفَلَقِ.....﴾

{Qul a'oodhu birabbil-falaq.....}[Surah Al-Falaq]

﴿قُلْ أَعُوذُ بِرَبِّ النَّاسِ.....﴾

{Qul a'oodhu birabbin-nas.....}[Surah An-Nas]

The Latecomer to the Prayer

He is the one that misses some parts, one rak'ah or more of the Prayer. So he completes whatever he has missed after the Imam has said the second *Tasleem* (concluding act of the prayer). The beginning of the latecomer's prayer is considered from where he started praying with the imam. He is considered to have prayed a *rak'ah* by catching the *ruku'* (bowing position) with the imam. But if he misses the bowing position with the *imam* he has missed that *rak'ah* as a whole.

The latecomer should join the congregation in whatever part of the prayer he finds them when he enters the mosque, whether they are standing, bowing, prostrating, and so on. He should not wait for them to stand up for the following *rak'ah*. He should say the opening *Takbeer* while standing, except for one with some excuse like the sick.

Things that nullify the prayer
1. Deliberate speech even though it was little.
2. Deviation from the direction of the *Qiblah* with all the body.
3. Occurrence of anything that vitiates the ablution.
4. Excessive and successive movements without necessity.
5. Laughing, even though it was little.
6. If he deliberately adds a bowing (*ruku'*) or prostration (*sujud*), or standing or sitting.
7. Deliberately preceding the imam.

Obligatory aspects (Wajibaat) of the prayer
1. All *takbeers* excluding the opening *takbeer* (*takbeeratul-Ihraam*).
2. To say: (سُبْحَانَ رَبِّيَ الْعَظِيم) - *subhana rabbiyal-'adheem*, once in the bowing position (*ruku'*).
3. To say: (سَمِعَ اللهُ لِمَنْ حَمِدَه) – *sami'Allahu liman hamidah*, with respect to the Imam and the one praying alone, when rising from the bowing position.
4. To say: (رَبَّنَا وَلَكَ الْحَمْدُ) - *Rabb-ana walakal-hamdu*, after rising from the bowing position.
5. To say: (سُبْحَانَ رَبِّيَ الأَعْلَى) - *subhana Rabbiyal a'la*, once in the prostration position (*sujood*).

6. To say: (رَبِّ اغْفِرْ لِي) – *Rabbigh firlee,* between the two prostrations.
7. The first *tashahhud.*
8. Sitting for the first *tashahhud.*

Basic elements (*Arkaan*) of the prayer

1. To stand, if able, during the obligatory prayers. Standing is not compulsory during the supererogatory prayers. The reward of praying sitting (in a voluntary prayer) is equivalent to half of the reward of praying standing.
2. *Takbeeratul ihraam;* the opening *takbeer.*
3. Reciting Surah Al-Fatihah in each *rak'ah.*
4. Bowing in each *rak'ah.*
5. Standing upright after rising from *ruku'* (bowing).
6. To prostrate with the seven parts of the body twice in each *rak'ah.*
7. Sitting between the two prostrations.
8. Observing tranquility in all the acts mentioned above.
9. The final *tashahhud.*
10. Sitting for the final *tashahhud.*
11. Invoking prayers and blessings of Allah upon the Prophet.
12. Saying the *tasleem* (concluding act of the prayer).
13. Maintaining the order between the basic elements of the Prayer.

Oversights in the Prayer

An oversight means a mistake or omission done unintentionally. When someone forgets or commits an oversight in his prayers by adding or decreasing from his prayers or when he thinks that he may have increased or decreased from it, then *sujud as-sahw* or the prostration of oversight is prescribed for him.

Also if he mistakenly adds a standing, bowing, or sitting, or the like to his prayer, he must prostrate two prostrations after *tasleem* to rectify the error he has committed.

Similarly, when he mistakenly reduces something from the prayer by leaving any action or word.

If the omitted word or action is a pillar (*Rukn*) and he remembers it before commencing recitation in the following *rak'ah*, he must return to perform the missing pillar or that basic element, then observe the other aspects following it, and then do the prostration of forgetfulness.

However, if he could not recollect it except after he has begun recitation in the following *rak'ah*, that particular *rak'ah* in which the omission occurred becomes void and the following *rak'ah* takes its place.

If he could not accomplish the forgotten *rukn* (basic element) except after the *tasleem,* but there has not been a long period between the prayer and the time he recollects, he should observe a full *rak'ah* and prostrate the prostration of forgetfulness. However, if there has been a long time gap or his ablution has been vitiated, he should repeat the whole prayer.

If he forgets an obligatory aspect of the prayer (*Wajib*) such as the sitting for the first tashahhud or the like, he should observe the two prostrations of forgetfulness before making the *tasleem.*

However, in case of nursing doubts about the number of rak'ahs observed like when he doubts whether he has observed two or three *rak'ahs,* he should consider the lower number and carry on therefrom. This is because he is certain about the lower number but he must observe the prostration of forgetfulness before making *tasleem.*

If he doubts having omitted a basic element (*rukn*), he should do as if he has actually omitted it by observing it and the other aspects following it and then observe the prostration of forgetfulness.

If he thinks that he is most likely to have done one of the two, then he should act according to the stronger probability and observe the prostration of forgetfulness.

The Recommended but Voluntary Prayers *(As-Sunan Ar-Rawatib)*[1]

It is a desirable act for every Muslim man and woman, to maintain the performance of twelve optional *rak'ahs* while being resident. These *rak'ahs* are four *rak'ahs* of optional prayers before *Zuhr* and two after the *Zuhr* (noon) prayer, and two after the *Maghrib* (evening) prayer, and two after the *'Isha'* (night) prayer and two before the *Subh* (dawn) prayer.

Umm Habibah (May Allah be pleased with her) reported: I heard the Messenger of Allah (May the blessings and peace of Allah be upon him) saying, **"A house will be built in Al-Jannah for every Muslim who offers twelve Rak'ah of optional *Salaah* other than the obligatory *Salaah* in a day and a night (to seek the Pleasure of Allah."** [Transmitted by Muslim: 728].

The best practice for a Muslim regarding *As-Sunan Ar-Rawatib*, and supererogatory prayers in general is to perform them at home. Jabir reported Allah's

---

(1) **As-Sunan Ar-Rawatib** implies thesteady and constant supererogatory prayers that are performed after the obligatory prayers. They are two or four optional *rak'ahs* prayed at specific times of the day and night. They are twelve *rak'ahs* in all according to the sounder opinion.

Messenger (May the blessings and peace of Allah be upon him) as saying: **"When any one of you observes prayer in the mosque, he should reserve a part of his prayer for his house, for Allah would make the prayer as a means of betterment in his house."** [Transmitted by Muslim: 778].

Moreover, it was reported in an agreed upon tradition on the authority of Zaid bin Thabit (May Allah be pleased with him) that the Prophet (May the blessings and peace of Allah be upon him) said, **"O people! Perform your (voluntary) *Salah* (prayers) in your homes because the best *Salah* of a man is the one he performs at home, except the obligatory *Salah*."** [Agreed upon: 6113, 781].

Al-Witr prayer

It is a Sunnah practice for a Muslim to perform *Al-Witr* prayer. It is an emphatic Sunnah whose time begins after the Isha (night) prayer and continues until dawn, though the best time to perform it is the last part of the night for one whois sure to rise up in the night.

It is of the supererogatory acts of worship that the Messenger of Allah (May the blessings and peace of Allah be upon him) never abandoned. He always performed it whether resident or on a journey.

The least number of *rak'ahs* for the *Witr* prayer is one *rak'ah*. The Messenger of Allah (May the blessings and peace of Allah be upon him) used to observe eleven *rak'ahs* in the night according to the tradition reported by Aisha (May Allah be pleased with her) that the Messenger of Allah (May the blessings and peace of Allah be upon him) used to pray eleven *rak'ahs* in the night, making them odd by a single one. [Transmitted by Muslim: 736].

The night prayer consists of pairs of *rak'ahs*. Ibn 'Umar (May Allah be pleased with him) reported that a person asked the Messenger of Allah (May the blessings and peace of Allah be upon him) about the night prayer. The Messenger of Allah (May the blessings and peace of Allah be upon him) said, **"Prayer during the night should consist of pairs of *rak'ahs*, but if one of you fear morning is near, he should pray one *rak'ah* which will make his prayer an odd number for him."** [Transmitted by Muslim: 749].

It is sometimes desirable for him to recite the *Qunoot* invocation after rising from the bowing position during the *Witr* prayer owing to the tradition narrated by Al-Hassan bin Ali (May Allah be pleased with both of them) where the Prophet (May the blessings and peace of Allah be upon him) taught him some words he should say during the *Witr* invocation. However, he should not make it a constant practice because a majority of those who described the Prophet's prayer did not mention his act of reciting *Qunoot* invocation.

It is also a desirable act for the one who missed the night optional prayer to make up for it during the day but with even number of rak'ahs by observing two, four, six, eight, ten or twelve *rak'ahs* according to the practice of the Prophet (May the blessings and peace of Allah be upon him) in this regard.

The Two Voluntary *Rak'ahs* of the *Fajr* Prayer

Two *rak'ahs* before the dawn *(Fajr)* prayer are part of the recommended but voluntary prayers that the Messenger of Allah (May the blessings and peace of Allah be upon him) used to maintain. He never abandoned them whether he was residing or travelling. 'Aishah (may Allah be pleased with her) reported saying, "The Prophet (May the blessings and peace of Allah be upon him) did not attach more importance to any supererogatory (*Nawafil*) prayer than the two rak'ahs of prayer before dawn (*Fajr*) prayer." [Agreed upon: 1163, 724].

Moreover, in their regard, the Messenger of Allah said, **"They are dearer to me than the whole world."** [Transmitted by Muslim: 725].

Taharah and Salah

It is an established practice (*sunnah*) of the Prophet (May the blessings and peace of Allah be upon him) to recite in the first *rak'ah*:

﴿ قُلْ يا أَيُّهَا الكافرون ..... ﴾

{*Qul ya ayyuhal-kafiroon...*} [Surah Al-Kafiroon]
And to recite:

﴿ قُلْ هُوَ اللهُ أَحَدٌ ..... ﴾

{*Qul huwa Allahu ahad...*}   [Surah Al-Ikhlas]
in the second *rak'ah*.

Sometimes, he would recite in the first rak'ah:

﴿ قُولُوا آمَنَّا بِالله وَمَا أُنْزِلَ إِلَيْنَا ...الآية ﴾ . [البقرة:١٣٦]،

{*Quloo aamanna billahi wa ma unzila ilaina...*} [Surah Al-Baqarah: 136]
And in the second *rak'ah*:

﴿ قُلْ يَا أَهْلَ الْكِتَابِ تَعَالَوْا إِلَى كَلِمَةٍ سَوَاءٍ بَيْنَنَا وَبَيْنَكُمْ ... الآية ﴾ [آل عمران:٦٤]

{*Qul ya ahl al-kitabi ta'aalaw ila kalimatin sawa'in bainana wa bainakum...*} [Surah Aal-Imran: 64].

It is also the *sunnah* to keep them short, according to the practice of the Prophet (may the blessings and peace of Allah be upon him). One who misses praying them before *fajr* may perform them after the prayer. However, it is preferable to perform them after sunrise when the shadows begin to appear (15 minutes after sunrise approximately) until shortly before the prohibited time for prayer when the sun passes the meridian (*Zawalus-Shams*).

Ad-Dhuha (Forenoon) Prayer

This is the prayer of the penitent (*Al-Awwabeen*). It is an emphatic and confirmed Sunnah, whose encouragement has been emphatically reported in several traditions.

Abu Dharr (May Allah be pleased with him) reported that the Messenger of Allah (May the blessings and peace of Allah be upon him) said, *"When you get up in the morning, charity is due from every one of your joints. There is charity in every ascription of glory to Allah; there is charity in every declaration of His Greatness; there is charity in every utterance of praise of Him; there is charity in every declaration that He is the only true God (worthy of worship); there is charity in enjoining good; there is charity in forbidding evil. Two rak'ahs of Duha (Forenoon prayer) is equal to all this (in reward)."* [Reported by Muslim: 720].

It was narrated that Abu Hurairah (May Allah be pleased with him) said: *"My dearest friend advised me (to do) three things: to fast three days each month, to pray two rak'ahs of Duha prayer, and to sleep after praying witr."* [Agreed upon: 1178, 721].

Taharah and Salah

The best time to observe this prayer is when the sun has risen (i.e. later in the day) and its heat has become intense. Its time expires upon *Zawalus-Shams* (when the sun has declined and passed the meridian). The minimum number of *rak'ahs* for *Ad-Duha* prayer is two *rak'ahs* and there is no limit for the maximum.

Prohibited Times of Prayer

There are times in which prayer is not permissible, namely:

1. After *Fajr* prayer until the sun rises to the height of a spear (approximately 15 minutes after sunrise).
2. When the sun reaches zenith at noon (when the shadow reaches its lowest point), until it begins to set. (Approximately 10 minutes before the beginning of the time of *Dhuhr*).
3. After *Asr* prayer, until sunset.

However, some prayers may be performed during the prohibited times such as prayers with special reasons like the *tahiyyatul-Masjid* (two *rak'ahs* said upon entering the mosque), funeral prayer, eclipse prayer, two *rak'ahs* of *Tawaf*, two *rak'ahs* of ablution and the likes.

It is also permissible to make up for the missed obligatory prayers at these times because the Prophet

(May the blessings and peace of Allah be upon him) said, *"He who forgets any prayer, or he slept (and it was omitted), his expiation is (only) that he should observe it when he remembers it."* [Agreed upon: 597, 684].

One may also make up for the dawn (*Fajr*) supererogatory prayer. It is also permissible to pay back the *Dhuhr* supererogatory prayer after *Asr* for anyone who missed it at its time.

www.ingramcontent.com/pod-product-compliance
Lightning Source LLC
LaVergne TN
LVHW020444080526
838202LV00055B/5332